TO ACHIEVE EVERYTHING BEING LAZY

by LINKED IN AND TOWN HALL ACHIEVER OF THE YEAR
EY NOMINEE ENTREPRENEUR OF THE YEAR
GRAND HOMAGE LYS DIVERSITY
WORLD TOP100 DOCTORS

Dr BAK NGUYEN, DMD

TO ALL THE MILLENNIALS LOOKING
TO WIN BIG IN LIFE AND TO HAVE IT ALL

by Dr BAK NGUYEN

Copyright © 2021 Dr BAK NGUYEN

All rights reserved.

ISBN: 978-1-989536-71-1

Published by: Dr. BAK PUBLISHING COMPANY
Dr.BAK 0090

DISCLAIMER

« The general information, opinions and advice contained in this medium and/or the books, audiobooks, podcasts and publications on Dr. Bak Nguyen's (legal name Dr. Ba Khoa Nguyen) website or social media (hereinafter the "Opinions") present general information on various topics. The Opinions are intended for informational purposes only.

No information contained in the Opinions is a substitute for an expert, consultation, advice or diagnosis. No information contained in the Opinions is a substitute for professional advice and should not be construed as consultation or advice.

Nothing in the Opinions should be construed as professional advice related to the practice of dentistry, medical advice or any other form of legal or financial advice, professional opinion, care or diagnosis, but strictly as general information. All information from the Opinions is for informational purposes only.

Any user who disagrees with the terms of this Disclaimer should immediately cease using or referring to the Opinions. Any action by the user in connection with the information contained in the Opinions is solely at the user's discretion.

The general information contained in the Opinions is provided "as is" and without warranty of any kind, either expressed or implied. Dr. Bak Nguyen (legal name Dr. Ba Khoa Nguyen) makes every effort to ensure that the information is complete and accurate. However, there is no guarantee that the general information contained in the Opinions is always available, truthful, complete, up-to-date or relevant.

The Opinions expressed by Dr. Bak Nguyen (legal name Dr. Ba Khoa Nguyen) are personal and expressed in his own name and do not reflect the opinions of his companies, partners and other affiliates.

Dr. Bak Nguyen (legal name Dr. Ba Khoa Nguyen) also disclaims any responsibility for the content of any hyperlinks included in the Opinions.

Always seek the advice of your expert advisors, physicians or other qualified professionals with any questions you may have regarding your condition. Never disregard professional advice or delay in seeking it because of something you have read, seen or heard in the Opinions. »

ABOUT THE AUTHOR

From Canada, **Dr. BAK NGUYEN**, Nominee Ernst and Young Entrepreneur of the year, Grand Homage Lys DIVERSITY, LinkedIn & TownHall Achiever of the year and TOP 100 Doctors 2021. Dr Bak is a cosmetic dentist, CEO and founder of Mdex & Co. His company is revolutionizing the dental field. Speaker and motivator, he wrote 72 books over 36 months accumulating many world records (to be officialized). His books are covering:

- **ENTREPRENEURSHIP**
- **LEADERSHIP**
- **QUEST OF IDENTITY**
- **DENTISTRY AND MEDICINE**
- **PARENTING**
- **CHILDREN'S BOOKS**
- **PHILOSOPHY**

In 2003, he founded Mdex, a dental company upon which in 2018, he launched the most ambitious private endeavour to reform the dental industry, Canada wide. Philosopher, he has close to his heart the quest of happiness of the people surrounding him, patients and colleagues alike. In 2020, he launched an International collaborative initiative named **THE ALPHAS** to share knowledge and for Entrepreneurs and Doctors to thrive through the Greatest Pandemic and Economic depression of our time.

In 2016, he co-found with Tranie Vo, Emotive World Incorporated, a tech research company to use technology to empower happiness and sharing. U.A.X. the ultimate audio experience is the landmark project on which the team is advancing, utilizing the technics of the movie industry and the advancement in ARTIFICIAL INTELLIGENCE to save the book industry and to upgrade the continuing education space.

These projects have allowed Dr Nguyen to attract interests from the international and diplomatic community and he is now the center of a global discussion in the wellbeing and the future of the health profession. It is in that matter that he shares his thoughts and encourages the health community to share their own stories.

"It's not worth it go through it alone! Together, we stand, alone, we fall."

Motivational speaker and serial entrepreneur, philosopher and author, from his own words, Dr Nguyen describes himself as a dentist by circumstances, an entrepreneur by nature and a communicator by passion.

He also holds recognitions from the Canadian Parliament and the Canadian Senate.

TO ACHIEVE EVERYTHING BEING LAZY

by Dr BAK NGUYEN

INTRODUCTION
BY Dr BAK NGUYEN

CHAPTER 1
TO BE A REALISTIC OR TO BE A DREAMER?
Dr. BAK NGUYEN

CHAPTER 2
CAN YOU STILL BE LAZY AND RESILIENT AT THE SAME TIME?
Dr. BAK NGUYEN

CHAPTER 3
HOW TO EVALUATE RISK AND HOW TO SMELL TROUBLE FROM MILES AWAY?
Dr. BAK NGUYEN

CHAPTER 4
I GOT THE SALARY, NOW WHAT?
Dr. BAK NGUYEN

CHAPTER 5
HOW TO CHALLENGE YOUR NEGATIVE THOUGHTS?
Dr. BAK NGUYEN

CHAPTER 6
WHAT ABOUT EGO? CAN YOU LEVERAGE THAT TOO?
Dr. BAK NGUYEN

CHAPTER 7
HOW TO LOVE AND GROW?
Dr. BAK NGUYEN

CHAPTER 8
HOW TO DEFEND YOURSELF FROM MANIPULATIVE PEOPLE?
Dr. BAK NGUYEN

CONCLUSION
BY Dr BAK NGUYEN

INTRODUCTION
by Dr. BAK NGUYEN

I am writing these words as LAZY volume 1: **THE CONFESSION OF A LAZY OVERACHIEVER** just got released in 51 countries from Apple Books, less than 12 hours ago. It got released without any fireworks nor celebrations.

This was not because I did not care, actually, I love that new angle to share information and secrets with a younger audience, it did not receive any celebration because I was too busy and lazy to give it any. That will be Jamies's job.

This morning, I was torn between starting the 2nd volume of LAZY, this one, or to finish my other opened projects. Then, as I decided to go with my feelings, I finally decided to keep my focus on the new franchise, LAZY to leverage my emotional intelligence. You see, this is how I am celebrating, with you, the release of one book, writing another one.

> "AND SO, BUSY AND LAZY BECAME ONE."
> Dr. BAK NGUYEN

My joy, my pride, my endorphins, I put them to good use, furthering my momentum. As I sat down with my laptop, I was again torn between 2 questions: do I start writing the new chapter, or do I finished editing the first volume for Amazon and Barnes & Noble?

All of my teachers will be saying to finish a task first and then, start a new one. "If you start too many projects, you may finish none…" and usually, they will be right. But editing films, I learnt how faulty and flaw that model was.

In my first movie, **QUESTION OF PERCEPTION**, I edited the whole movie about 70 times. I was learning on the field, the technics, the software, the requirements while developing the mindset and the vision. I was about in my 40th version when it got released in theatre for the first time.

Each scene has a clean-cut, both in storyline and emotions. The accumulation of the scenes pushed the storyline forward. It was painful to watch. Not because the movie was bad, but because at every 7 to10 minutes, we checked out and checked back in again. The public was kind enough to share their impression with me and I learnt much from that premiere.

I went back to the editing room and cut most of the ending scenes of each scene. Then, I had to work on my transitions, so it does not feel like we are moving from scene to scene but smoothly throughout the entire movie. That took me another 30 more versions… Doing that, I learnt much about how our minds work.

> "TO EASE IN, ANYWHERE AND IN ANYTHING, IS THE MOST DIFFICULT TASK SINCE WE NEED MOTIVATION AND FIGHTING AGAINST RESISTANCE WITHOUT ANY VELOCITY."
>
> Dr. BAK NGUYEN

I came to see my life as a big movie. I do not get from one scene to the next since it takes too much energy and motivation just to go through my days. Instead, I use the *velocity* of a scene to propel me into the next scene of my life.

Looking back at my life, I have a long never-ending story that keeps growing in intrigues and actions. Writing books is my way to edit them, to edit my life. I then have to look back and decide on a starting point and an ending one. Most of the time, the celebrations happened much, much later, as my team finally joins in.

For those of you who know me and met me at one of these celebrations, I am always a little off, busy with, not the celebrations nor the completion of that project, but I have my head and heart completely immersed in my next project already.

This is one of the main reasons why, almost 4 years after the fact, I still haven't remove the *"to be officialized"* in front of my world records announcements. Sure, it is high on my to-do list, but each time, jumping headfirst into my next book and adventure is much more appealing to me. Appealing and fun.

So to me, celebrating with fireworks and a banquet the release of LAZY was not a priority anyway. And we are in COVID times, celebrations happened alone or online anyway. This could have depressed many of you. Not me, I was going online anyway!

Back to the editing of my book and writing my next chapter, I went from writing my next chapter, because it was easier to jump to the project than to motivate myself to edit. This is no fun in editing. So as I finish this chapter, announcing to the world that volume 1 will be released on Amazon and Barnes & Nobles soon, I am forcing my own hand to skip the *motivation and procrastination* phase.

One precision here. Have you noticed that I used writing my next chapter, not starting my next book? Why do you think I was talking like that? To not check-out and then, have to check back in.

> "MOTIVATION IS SOMETHING YOU NEED TO BEGIN. ONCE IN ACTION, VELOCITY AND DEDICATION WILL KEEP YOU UP, NOT MOTIVATION."
> Dr. BAK NGUYEN

And with this, we are coming back to the motivation chapter in our previous journey. How is this for an introduction? We pick up right where we left. And why make it into 2 volumes instead of one? Well, just like you, I have a short attention span.

Volume 1 finished with 18,861 words. It is a respectable book and yet, thin enough to ease you in the reading. How many times did you pick up a book with a great title that promised much, to end up putting it back on the shell because it was too thick?

> "TO EASE IN IS THE BEST APPROACH THEN TO HAVE TO CHECK-IN. AND ONCE IN, DO NOT CHECK-OUT."
> Dr. BAK NGUYEN

Using that metaphor, do you remember how you felt the last time that you were checking-in at the hotel? You might be excited about being at the hotel but checking-in was not the best of experience. You couldn't wait to get to your room, to change to go to the beach or to have sex!

Standing in the lounge as they prepare your room was just part of the deal. It even increases your pleasure as you were thinking of fun and sex while smiling back at the hotel clerk, while hiding your true thoughts.

That's fine, it even has a charm of its own. Now, imagine having to do that each time you need to access your room. How would that feel? One check-in and make it as pleasant as possible. Then, try to skip the check-out and ease your way into your next adventure…

And with this, I just realized that I just signed my introduction to the 2nd volume of LAZY: **TO OVERACHIEVE EVERYTHING BEING LAZY.** With me, you went to the steps and the emotions of how on a Monday morning at 8 AM I found the motivation to score yet, another adventure. This is about being lazy, I skipped the *motivation/procrastination* cycle.

Then, I put the pressure on myself to deliver, so as soon as I will be finishing this chapter, I will jump right into the editing of the first volume. Time-wise, as the first volume will be done and reached Amazon, I might be at the 3rd or 4th chapter within this book. That celebration will keep me going.

Then, by my 5th or 6th chapter, Barnes and Noble should be announcing my new release too. This will be another victory and the energy of the celebration will carry me to the finish line of the present volume.

Actually, it is not exactly true. But having to motivate myself to edit my book while keeping the inspiration and energy to write more and more chapters is a huge challenge on its own.

Whatever energy and goodwill I am spending on editing, I make sure that it will propel me on everything else I have on my plate. I do not need the motivation to write but I welcome the recognition of having my books released by prestigious partners to keep feeding my vibe. And this is how I became and maintained an *overachiever status*.

I can't promise that I will make all of you into overachievers. What I will promise is that you will share my daily and journey and comprehend its logic and steps. From the outside, it might feel intimidating since you are looking at the celebrations and the gossip after the facts.

> "TRUST ME, WHEN YOU STAND RIGHT IN THE MIDDLE OF THE STORM, IT IS CALM AND SIMPLE."
> Dr. BAK NGUYEN

This is **TO OVERACHIEVE EVERYTHING BEING LAZY**, the second volume of the LAZY franchise. Welcome to the Alphas.

CHEAT YOUR WAY TO SUCCESS
Dr. BAK NGUYEN

CHAPTER 1
TO BE A REALISTIC OR TO BE A DREAMER?

"ENJOY YOUR DREAMS FIRST, ONLY THEN, YOU MAY ENGAGE AND EMPOWER THEM."

BY DR. BAK NGUYEN

While I am at it, why not? Let jump right to the next question, to be realistic or to be a dreamer? If in the first journey, my goal was to ease you in the mindset, in this second volume, let's leverage over what we learnt to start overachieving. To learn and to understand are just the beginning of the journey, one still has to walk the path.

So what does that mean to be *realistic*? In common terms, it is to set a reasonable goal and to do your best to get it done in time. You will set a goal within your sight and will increment small steps to reach that goal. This is a miss conception of victory, even if all of the parts of the equation were true, the context was falsely applied.

To aim for something within reach is surely a good start. To increment small steps is your only way to get things done. So what is missing? You have a great tactic of how to move forward but no vision. You can't get anywhere worthy if all you are aiming for what is already within reach.

In other words, how can you expect to grow if you are safe within your comfort zone? And here it is, this is often where I usually lose people. Very few are ready to leave their comfort zone. Is there any way to grow beyond without leaving the comfort zone? Absolutely, it is call dreaming!

Dream and as you do not limit yourself to dream of new horizons, new people, new food, new friends, new adventures, why is it that you feel safe? Because you are doing so without fear of judgment nor the pressure to deliver on any of these desires and fantasies. This isn't bad, it is the vision.

> **"ENJOY YOUR DREAMS FIRST, ONLY THEN, YOU MAY ENGAGE AND EMPOWER THEM."**
> Dr. BAK NGUYEN

To visit desires and horizons beyond your sight wasn't that hard, everybody is doing it. Unfortunately, it's not that true. We should read that everyone does that somewhere in their life. Some still do, others have given up. Why, why would someone stop dreaming? Because the awaking back to reality was too painful.

The bigger and crazier the dream, the harder the awakening. This is no secret to anyone. I can tell you to believe in your dreams and to work hard. I can tell you to never give up on your dreams because those are the real you. I can tell you to fight for what you believe. Where will all of these leads? Usually, to empower your desires for a few days before the fire fades and you are back to reality.

So I won't tell you any of these things. Instead, I will ask you, if dreaming was so fun, why even bother to come back to reality? Before you answer that one, please ask yourself the question loudly and listen to your words and your voice. Then, answer and listen with even more attention to your answers. Was that you talking or your parents, teachers, and all the figures of **Conformity** etched within you?

You want to be lazy? You want to have fun? Well, you felt good dreaming, keep dreaming!

> "TO BE REALISTIC MEANS, BY DEFINITION, TO COME BACK TO A LESSER WORLD THAN THOSE YOU WERE DREAMING OF."
> Dr. BAK NGUYEN

I taught you to use your emotions as *triggers*. What did you feel dreaming? We all dream about what we do not have, what we are not, yet, and things that haven't happened yet. In some cultures and civilizations, those are called visions. And the magic was that you felt safe the whole time, dreaming is within your comfort zone, otherwise, you would not be dreaming!

Can you see the *hack*? We just realized a way to have vision without having to stretch our comfort zone. What was the feeling? Happiness, empowerment, and freedom are usually the answers. Use those feelings as *triggers* to kickstart your hormones to react. If you do so quickly, your mind won't have the time to snap back to reality before your body starts to react to the surge of hormones.

Then, keeping in mind to be lazy, what would be easier? To use your goodwill to contain that energy looking to be expressed or to go with it? Once again, do not release that energy within your cell, your room, and some close enclaves full of people and of rules. Do so in a larger environment, one in which your emotions and yourself are free to move and to explore. This is step one.

We all know that the hormones will fade out, sooner or later. So then what? You will have 2 choices: either to resume to reality and to walk back in your enclaves and cells or to face the consequences of your decisions.

> "PERSONALLY, I HATE TO COME BACK TO MY FOOTSTEPS, SO I MOVE FORWARD."
> Dr. BAK NGUYEN

I will not tell you what to do, that's your decision to make. Whatever your decision, you can only keep going or decide to come back to reality. Just know that going back to reality is a *long walk*, one without any fun. On the way, regrets are paving each inch. That is usually why people stop dreaming, that walk, they knew and sore never to walk again, *the walk of remorses*.

Before you make up your mind, let's explore the second option, to move forward. I won't lie, this path is even longer than the first one. It is longer and we have no way to know how long nor how hard it would be. So here too, there is pain, only there can also be much gain.

> "LOOKING BACK, THERE IS PAIN AND THE INSURANCE OF NO GAIN. LOOKING FORWARD AT LEAST, YOU HAVE THE HOPE OF GAIN. WHAT WILL COUNTERBALANCE IS FEAR AND YOUR PERCEPTION OF IT."
> Dr. BAK NGUYEN

And this is what it boils down to: *fear*. Fear of the unknown. You will be surprised how resilient one can be to pain. It is to fear that most people will dodge and give up. And what is *fear*? A sensation maintained alive with hormones. And what do we now know about hormones? It is an *all-or-nothing* reaction.

In other words, you will experience *fear* if that was the only feeling available or the strongest one. Going out from your dream, was it fear that kept you going? No, it was empowerment, happiness, and freedom! Use any of those as *triggers* and you will keep fear at bay.

The best way to do that was to get out of your head and to feel. By feeling how your body reacts as you feel empowerment, happiness, or freedom, you will follow the path of less resistance, to give in to it! This was about leveraging your laziness, remember?

So no more *fear*, at least for a little while. And we all know that the hormonal effect will be fade eventually. So how to keep moving forward before fear comes knocking? Well, it is to aim for the next small win. What you call being *realistic* but not as a vision but as a **how-to**.

As you are aiming for a small win within reach, you will score it quickly. What you do think happens as you score? Your body react with hormones, not those of *fear* but those of the *victor*. Your **Confidence** will rise.

> "WITH CONFIDENCE, YOU ARE SILENCING DOUBTS AND KEEPING FEAR AT THE GATE."
> Dr. BAK NGUYEN

With each win, as they keep coming in, you have managed to maintain a steady (or almost) flow of hormones to keep you going. It is a little like having a car to self-regenerate its fuel as it is moving faster.

This car has not been invented yet but the principle is well known: either you need an infinite source of energy or your need to overcome the resistance facing you. In space, there is no resistance, a body will keep moving.

Let's be *realistic* to use your wording, for now, let's find a way to refuel on the way and that is to move from one small win to the next, daily. To keep going since energy is scarce, you do not want to waste it on checking-in and out, so use your celebration to ease your way into your next win.

Doing so, you will be halfway through as these hormones run out. Then the sight of the arrival line will push you to go the *extra mile*. And this is how you overachieve.

So no, it is not a good thing to limit yourself right at the start being *realistic*. Use that *realistic* mindset to keep the wins coming to fuel your journey, just as I described mine in the introduction. And, by all means, dream. Dream as much as you want and as crazy as you desire. Then, seize your emotions as *triggers* and see what happens.

Remember, to keep going, it was either to have no friction (so do not step on other people's toes, that's the best way to generate a wall of friction, even opposition) or to keep refuelling yourself as you keep going forward, a win after the next will do that.

This is **TO OVERACHIEVE EVERYTHING BEING LAZY**, the second volume of the LAZY franchise. Welcome to the Alphas.

CHEAT YOUR WAY TO SUCCESS
Dr. BAK NGUYEN

CHAPTER 2
CAN YOU STILL BE LAZY AND RESILIENT AT THE SAME TIME?

"GET RID OF ALL OF THE LABELS YOU HAVE BEEN GIVEN.
EVEN THOSE YOU'VE CREATED YOURSELF."

BY DR. BAK NGUYEN

Absolutely, you can be lazy and resilient at the same time! What screwed all of us is that **Conformity** labeled laziness as a bad thing. Somehow, in our culture, being resilient is also a synonym for putting our heads down to survive calamity and suffering.

Well, if keeping our head down and our hopes up is resiliency, that's not all of what resilience is. Resiliency is to be there and to get the job done no matter what. In bad times, resiliency is a synonym for survival and hard work. And why will you survive being resilient? You will become stronger while the others are hiding or looking to shift the blame, you are out there climbing out of the *hole*.

This is the archetype we all recognize as resiliency. But what about once out of the *hole*? Some will have exhausted their vital energy and resume to how they were. This happens when someone uses resiliency as an endgame. Being resilient is not a goal, it should not be a phase, but a nature. If you can keep up the pace even once out of the hole, now you stand a chance to thrive.

This would mean that everyone that have survived a war and immigration are huge successes? Unfortunately not, and here is why. Some, as soon as out of trouble will resume or even overcompensate on their pain, reversing back to their old habits. If the pain was significant, those will be the minority, if the pain was temporary and quick, most people will resume as they were before.

Let's get back to the idea of war and immigration. None will argue that those are light pain. So why all immigrants aren't super successful after such training, surviving war is surely an extreme selection process? Well, because they got stuck in the third gear, in surviving mode.

Whatever you experienced in life, it will change you, if not 180 degrees, it will still leave a mark. When war hit, people had to lay down and adapt. The lower their heads, the better the chance of survival.

At that altitude, the world is different and the rules also. They have successfully adapted and even escaped their condition. But some will be broken by the experience and will keep going in survival mode. They forgot what it was to thrive, and whatever new attitude they've learnt adapting, they lose, now failing to adapt to post-war conditions.

Please don't misunderstand me, I have the uttermost respect for these people who refuse to let go and fought for their future. My parents and grandparents are amongst these people. But then, as conditions change, as scarcity changes for opportunities, they missed on the next jump, abundance.

Out of respect, I will add that it is always easy to say if you never experienced the pain yourself, and on that, I am grateful. That being said, from a purely logical standpoint, adapting got them through war and immigration. Why stop there?

Actually, they never stopped. They will keep adapting and readapting, what they failed to do is looking back up, to the sky again. They have become a force of nature, moving forward no matter what. Even if they are not advancing in a day, in a week, in a month, they are resilient and won't stop pushing forward until they succeed or until they die.

A piece of advice, don't stand in the way of these people. This is the thread of what our champions, heroes, leaders, and millionaires are made from. So why the immigrants and war survivals are not all champions, heroes, or overachievers after the war, if they kept their aptitude? Because of their *aim*.

With the habit of keeping your head down to move forward, in what direction are you progressing? In the direction that you are looking at. If you were looking down, you will be moving in that direction. If you are moving up, it is because you broke the seal of the trauma and changed your trajectory, once more.

> "YOUR HEAD AND YOUR SIGHT DICTATE YOUR TRAJECTORY. KEEP YOUR HEAD UP."
> Dr. BAK NGUYEN

In most of my books, I said to let the heart lead and let the head follow. Well, have I just said the opposite? Absolutely not, there are no hormones and no emotions in your head, just filters, and conditioning (**memory**), so no *triggers* either.

Learning about the war survivors, their desire to live was in their hearts, not their heads. That was their only way to keep the hopes up with the odds stacking against them. Then, they kept their heads down as a tactic to make it through the day. Their vision was still to survive.

So they have hope (heart and desire) first and leverage their head to success. Heart first and then head second. Once out of the war, the desire has been filled, now they need to replace that with a desire as strong to keep their aptitude.

Most will be too tired and as they will face the new conditions of existence, even at peace, will stay in their heads. They have risked too much, now it is time to play it safe, or, at least, safer. So with that, they surrender hope and will be pushing forward with tactic alone (**head**), lacking vision (**hope**).

"CONFIDENCE IS SEXY"
Dr. BAK NGUYEN

And this is why it is so important to look in the mirror to remind us of who we are and what we want. Only from your heart and body can you generate emotions to use as *triggers*.

Only your body will produce hormones in reaction. Your head will empower you to restrain the message from the rest of your body. We can spend a lifetime mastering our heads, but this was about laziness!

Let your heart dictate the vision (*hopes, desires*) and spare yourself the denial or control of your hormones. Since you were the one triggering your body, you are already in control, just ride the *storm*, because make no mistake, this is what's coming, a *storm*. This is the power you have within you, all of us!

So being resilient does not mean surviving. It means to be there each day, day after day. That's a how-to. One still needs the vision to know where to go. In other words, one needs hope and desire to *trigger* his or her body to move forward.

And yes, being lazy can also help. Not by giving up, lazy never meant to sit on your hands doing nothing, just like resilience does not mean to survive. Those were just parts of reality.

> "LAZY DOES NOT MEAN YOU DO NOT HAVE TO DO SHIT, BUT THAT YOU DON'T HAVE TO GO THROUGH SHIT TO GET THINGS DONE."
> Dr. BAK NGUYEN

In the same line of thoughts, resilience doesn't me to keep your head down, but to go through whatever it takes (even *shit*) to reach the other shore. A little each day, day after day, that's resiliency.

Now, won't you mind a cheat? Actually, it is not a cheat but it will help you as much. What happens to someone who shows up on the field every day doing the same thing again and again? Well, he or she is getting better at it! So even through *shit*, this too shall pass, eventually!

And once on the other shore? Don't try to forget what just happened? Look back (this is one of the rare times that I will tell you to look back) and see what you just survive through. This will build back up your Confidence and look forward and up, knowing that you have what it took to walk against the odds. And guess what? Keep pushing and the odds are slowly changing in your favor!

In all of my books, I said that to look back is self-destructive. Well, this is a special case. After a trauma, one risks being broken and never recover, even if he or she adapted to survive. Looking back once on the other shore will bring back all of the negative feelings and souvenirs but also one refutable fact: they have made it successfully!

Luck, determination, hard work, resilience, name it, it was a cocktail of circumstances but still, they had to go through it all. With **Humility** and **Confidence**, they can now be moving forward.

> "YES, HUMILITY AND CONFIDENCE CAN CO-EXIST!"
> Dr. BAK NGUYEN

For those of you interest in the secret of leveraging humility to success, I will invite you to look for my 51st book, **HUMILITY FOR SUCCESS**. This is not about labeling but about leveraging the states of mind and perceptions into mindset. And what is a mindset? Well, it is a template for lazy people to act and to react faster to the events and to life.

> "IF YOU WANT TO BE LAZY, GET RID OF ALL OF THE LABELS YOU HAVE BEEN GIVEN, EVEN THOSE YOU'VE CREATED YOURSELF."
> Dr. BAK NGUYEN

Just feel to know your heart and desire. Then, your body will be doing the rest, just be smart enough or lazy enough to not stand in the way of the *storm* of your hormonal response. That was about being lazy. Now about overachieving, learn to surf the *storm* you just released! You are in control, stay in control, with both Confidence and Humility!

Be kind, be Confident, be humble and chill!

This is **TO OVERACHIEVE EVERYTHING BEING LAZY**, the second volume of the LAZY franchise. Welcome to the Alphas.

CHEAT YOUR WAY TO SUCCESS
Dr. BAK NGUYEN

CHAPTER 3
HOW TO EVALUATE RISK AND HOW TO SMELL TROUBLE FROM MILES AWAY?

"TO SMELL TROUBLE MILES AWAY, LOOK AT THE PEOPLE, MILES AWAY."
BY DR. BAK NGUYEN

No matter how you decide to interpret this one, no one can predict the future, the even. What scientists and researchers can do is only to predict trends by looking at the past. They can tell you what will happen but not when it will happen.

So how are we predicting the weather, will you ask? Well, even predicting the weather, we are not predicting the future, simply extrapolating the evolution of a phenomenon that has already started. And this is where our knowledge and powers reach a limit, a hard one.

Because all of our sciences and knowledge are fact-based. Is this great? Well, it crystallizes us in reaction mode, always reacting **after the facts**. I am not saying that it is wrong, simply stating a fact.

> "WITH BOTH OUR FEET FIRMLY PLANTED IN THE PAST, THE FUTURE IS NOT THAT EASILY ACCESSIBLE. EVEN LESS CHANGEABLE."
> Dr. BAK NGUYEN

What is the alternative? Science is science and everything else will be called fiction. Ever heard of science-fiction? What is science-fiction but the vision of the future? And this is what is lacking vision is. Even in science-fiction, the visions are often an extrapolation of today's facts. Or those anyhow predicting our future? Most of the time, it was just good entertainment.

Let get back to the *weather* example. If we can extrapolate the future from reacting to a present event, why isn't that more useful? Because we can only see slow events emerging, most of the life-threatening ones happen faster than we can react!

It is something to predict how many millimeters of snow we should expect, it is something else to predict when and where the next earthquake will occur. We all remember what happened at the last Tsunami where millions of lives were lost.

That being said, it is not just our short sight (based on reacting) that is the problem. By predicting successful slow events, we develop the false security that science can predict the future, and that is making us cocky thinking that we are on top of the world. No one can predict the future.

With this in mind, let explore the weather a little deeper, shall we? Even if we cannot predict the big and important events, knowing the weather a few days or hours in advance is surely very helpful. How do they do that?

They look at a present phenomenon (*triggers*) and at the conditions (wind, rotation of the planet, etc...), and with that, if the trend stays the same, they have a very good idea of what will come next based on science and experience.

Well, in everyday life, at our level, sure the weather and the big cataclysms will affect our lives and unfortunately, we will have no alternative than to react, after the facts. And even then, are there any chances to get ahead? Well, the weather is, once again, our perfect example.

When a storm or an earthquake hits, the birds are feeling them before we, humans, do. They react to it, flying away from the epicentre of the storm or the earthquake. Other animals will be doing the same, all running away from the life-threatening event. Most of the time, we will never see the event beforehand but looking at the reaction of the animals should give us a great hint.

This is even dumber than studying the weather will you say since it is putting us another step behind in the reaction process. We are not reacting to the reaction of the animals. In the absolute you will be right, this put us even more behind but the laws of statistics will show us another angle.

Most of the time, life-threatening events are not what occurs the most frequently. Actually, based on the laws of statistics, an animal may die more from the stampede resulting from the general panic than from the earthquake itself (in not *extinction-level* events).

In other words, in an *extinction level* event, whatever you do, the chances are that you will be gone. To what use is it to even discuss such events? Now, the minor variations are of interest to us since we will most often survive those and they will happen frequently. So then, how to predict the future being lazy?

Well, study the herds and learn to recognize the sign. It will be of much better use to you than to study the science in itself. Study the herds (crowd) and how they perceive and react to any *trigger*.

> "AT AN INDIVIDUAL LEVEL, YOU MIGHT FIND MANY VARIANCES. GROUP THE VARIANCES AND YOU WILL DEFINE TRENDS."
> Dr. BAK NGUYEN

And out those trends back at the basis of our constitution, the **Fear and Greed scale** to understand how people will react. From that, we are humans and we have evolved. Our evolution has allowed us to create a *buffer zone* between **Greed** and **Fear**, and that *buffer zone* is called **Comfort zone**.

Well, the Comfort zone is regulating how long can we face change without reacting. In other words, how much change can we take before reacting. Needless to say that at the extinction-level event, we will be running for our lives but what about the other situations?

Well, first we will ignore the signs and hammer those too sensitive to the variation. A government jailed the first physician who pointed out the outbreak of COVID-19! The man will die in prison, trying to warn the world.

Then, we will resist the change thinking that it will pass. And as the bodies start dropping, the news will be sharing in matters of hours from network to network to create a herd reaction. The news can be true or not, at this stage, it does not matter anymore. The new reality is the reaction of the herd. And as soon as **Fear** hit, a *stampede* will begin.

> "WHATEVER YOUR REASONS, NEVER STAND IN THE WAY OF A STAMPEDE, YOU MIGHT FACE THE WORSE PART OF THE STORM."
> Dr. BAK NGUYEN

And as soon as **Fear** is involved, our *herd reaction* will amplify the *trigger*. The longer we were ignoring and *buffering* the *triggers*, the more violently we will be reacting. And once the stampede has started, it is either to join it, to avoid it, or to die facing it. This is the study of herds and crowds.

So your question was how to evaluate risks and how to smell trouble miles away. Well, at *extinction-level*, I cannot help you. At *weather level*, look at the herd, it will give you much insights to know what will happen next.

If what you are looking to *smell* is smaller, just zoom into the size of the crowd you are studying. The smaller the size of your test group, the more variances you will find.

"TRENDS ARE ALWAYS TRUE AND TRENDS HAPPEN WITH NUMBERS, BIG NUMBERS."
Dr. BAK NGUYEN

For example, can you predict the stocks market? Can anyone? Some will say that it will crash. And they will right after the facts but never they will nail the exact timing of that crash. But once the crash initiates, everyone will be rushing for the doors, dropping the price by an X factor, this is what a crash is!

The only thing you can do is to know that it will happen. When is not a luxury you have unless you are the one crashing the market yourself! Understanding how the other people will react drafts a map of that future as it unveils. The question now is how will you react? If you have a plan in place, you might avoid being caught in the herd and victim of the *stampede*.

There are no good answers nor preparation to the situations above but as one gets prepare, one can see the stampede coming (after the crash) and have slightly more time to react.

The gain in time is the *buffer zone* being replaced with a **plan**. Remember that the *buffer zone* was a zone of denial? The other advantage you will have is that you are making your plans while not running from the storm, you have access to more of your faculties and aptitudes.

> "TO SMELL TROUBLE MILES AWAY, LOOK AT THE PEOPLE, MILES AWAY."
> Dr. BAK NGUYEN

Now, what about risk? This morning, I woke up reading a quote on my social wall. It says that one should have 2 lives, one to learn and one to live. That made me think, what is living but learning? What can you expect of a life where you have seen it all? One in which you know all of the pitfalls and the upsides. Is that life even worth of be living?

In other words, life is opportunity, the greatest of opportunities. Opportunities and risks and the exact same thing, just 2 faces of the same coin. Running away from risk is to refrain yourself from *life*. This is as true as embracing opportunity, you are embracing the chance of *dying*.

The point is to understand who you are and what are your *triggers*. Embrace those, even if all the odds are against you, that was your chance to happiness, freedom, and living. The *triggers* that aren't "*talking*" to you, try to avoid them, those are the problems you don't want to get caught in.

As you are jumping into your selection of problems, jump first, and then, leverage your hormones from the **flight or**

fight response, leverage your head to grow out of these troubles. Successfully doing so, you can then do it again and again, getting better at the game time after time.

A piece of advice, do not ask for opinions before or while you are jumping. Since you are jumping into your *selection of problems* (opportunity), to everyone else, it will just seem that you are crazy, looking for problems, they will never see the opportunity.

Those who will, are the ones that have the expertise to help you out once you are in. They will be selling you their expertise. And no, they aren't opportunists but the professionals and allies you will meet and trust to outgrow your problem and your previous self.

Know who you are first, that is the only way to understand your *selection of problems*, those are your *triggers*. As you know who you are, you can now differentiate between an opportunity and a problem. Jump headfirst in your opportunity and leverage your hormones and head to outgrow the hole you just jump in.

"JUMPING FROM HOLES TO HOLES,
YOU WILL BE TRAVELING MOUNTAINS."

Dr. BAK NGUYEN

And this is the essence of life, to live, to learn. Enjoy your journey.

This is **TO OVERACHIEVE EVERYTHING BEING LAZY**, the second volume of the LAZY franchise. Welcome to the Alphas.

CHEAT YOUR WAY TO SUCCESS
Dr. BAK NGUYEN

CHAPTER 4
I GOT THE SALARY, NOW WHAT? SHOULD I BUY 500 000 CUPS OF STARBUCK OR A HOUSE?

"STOP CHOOSING ONE OR THE OTHER. BE LAZY AND TAKE THEM BOTH! CHOOSING CAN BE EXHAUSTING!"
BY DR. BAK NGUYEN

This is such a great question to leverage laziness. Let's clear something, if your salary is $500,000 you are pretty smart and have proven your worth. That being said, what should you do with that money? The first thing you should do is to reinvest in yourself. Whatever makes you feel good, you should spoil yourself first.

And this is an unorthodox approach to this matter. Most people will tell you to work hard and to save. I won't tell you what to do. What I will tell you is what I would be doing in your shoes. Just to clear it out, this is true no matter your salary is $500,000, $50,000 or even $10,000.

I am lazy, that you know by now, so I will looking for the shortest way out of this, with results, of course. The worse thing to do here is to sabotage myself, if I have established my worth at half a million, whatever I did until now, I need to keep going. In my situation, it was to keep being a dentist operating at the chair.

> "STOP CHOOSING ONE OR THE OTHER. BE LAZY AND TAKE THEM BOTH! CHOOSING CAN BE EXHAUSTING!"
> Dr. BAK NGUYEN

This mentally will not work in all aspects of your life... you know what I am talking about. But in your career, this will have the advantage to keep your momentum going and allow you to build a second layer on top of that momentum (gaining in speed).

So get your cup of Starbuck if that keeps you happy. Being happy, you can then use that as a trigger to leverage your hormones. I will spend to reach happiness and confidence. But as soon as I have the feeling, I will leverage on those to keep producing more.

What of the lazy way? Actually, it was the easy way out. I would be successful but I will also be working harder and harder since I am exchanging my time for money. One can be as smart as possible, he or she will still have only 24 hours a day to trade.

And that is not even all! A salary is the most taxable income in most countries. In Canada where I am from, with a salary of half a million, the government will take more or less half of that money already. In other words, I can work twice as hard, I am losing half of it in taxes.

Is that fair? It is legal. But from the same legal system, there are other classes of income that are taxed less (capital gain and dividends for example). Well, guess what? As I studied the fiscal system, I realize that those income classes are not just less taxed, it also required less of my time!

> "THERE IS NO FREE MONEY IN LIFE.
> THERE IS EASIER AND HARDER MONEY THOUGH."
>
> Dr. BAK NGUYEN

Have I just stumbled upon a magical formula? Almost. To generate capital gains or dividends, I need to invest my hard-earned money. What I am exchanging for profit is the risk that I am taking, not my time anymore. The risk I will take is to lose my investment. This isn't something to take lightly.

And then, it is not all. To ensure that I put all the odds in my favour, I still need to understand what I am investing my money in. So I have to study again, not just in what to invest but also in that financial system and the players that I am playing against.

Only once I have understood the system, will I have a chance to win. So my ledger now is my invested capital and the time to study yet another system.

This is much work for a lazy person will you say, and I will agree. But here comes the upside. My alternative was to keep working, exchanging my time for a salary doing something I am good at. I still need to spend on that cup of coffee to keep me going.

Well, instead of drinking that cup of coffee to get me back at my job, I am drinking that cup of coffee to motivate me to push myself to evolve in a new system. It will take weeks and weeks of studying... so even more coffee!

Even if that is a joke, it is all true. I will be *spoiling* myself and leveraging that, doing something I won't be doing naturally. If that *cup of coffee is travelling*, well, I will be doing just that, to travel. I will also use all of the free time in transit to further my evolution (time in transit and waiting in line).

About travelling, I must add that travelling forces us to be open to readapt to our new environment. You can't do anything about that openness, it is how we are all built. Well, that was your chance to evolve! If you cross that window of openness learning boring systems, you just beat procrastination and inefficiency all at once.

If all you needed was a coffee, that's fine too. Whatever makes you feel happy, do it, for as long as you are not stepping on anyone else's toes, by all means, *indulge* yourself!

So I found a way to leverage my first success to pay for my time *indulging* myself. I then, leverage that *feeling-good vibe* to further my evolution. Well, guess what, within a few coffees and trips, I became much smarter without having to choose to change my life around. Actually, I did change it, I took the time to indulge myself!

What I learnt were finance and taxation systems. Then I started to invest. I learnt on the field and made my mistakes. By the way, the only true way to learn is to get your feet wet. Success in finance and investments (those that will generate capital gains and dividends) is not dictated by skill but by mindsets. In other words, it is about how you managed your emotions on the ground.

So I made my classes learning on the field. I know, this sounds like a lot of work, tell that to a lazy guy! What did you do today to learn? You have to spend time and money (tuitions) to master the desired skillset. Well, I did spend time and money learning and investing. Guess what? I eventually generate enough profit to cover all of my tuition fees and I am still coming out ahead with profit.

In simple words, I got paid to learn new ways to generate money. Add to that the taxation advantages, I still pay my fair share of taxes but since those are now dividends or capital gains, I got legally taxed at a much lower rate!

Let's me summarize this. I did paid and spend time learning new systems. I did that spoiling myself with coffee and travelling. Then, because the only way to really learn was to get my feet wet, I invested and kept learning on the way. I eventually make enough profit to cover all of my tuition fees and was still ahead with profit. I got paid to learn! And then, what do you think that I did? I repeat the whole process without the tuition fees, so even more profits!

I may have worked a little harder for a little while but a few years down the road, today, I generate more money working less while being taxed at a lower rate. How about that kind of laziness?

> "BEING LAZY DOESN'T MEAN THAT YOU DO NOT HAVE TO DO SHIT, IT MEANS THAT YOU DO NOT HAVE TO GO THROUGH SHIT TO GET THINGS DONE!"
>
> Dr. BAK NGUYEN

So once again, I am not telling you what to do or what not to do. I am simply sharing with you what I did and why. Please validate your plan with your advisors (accountants and lawyers) before doing any kind of investment. But what I can tell you is that if you give yourself enough time to learn and to get your feet wet, you will come out ahead eventually!

And one last thing? I never gave up my day job either! Today I am still a dentist that people are looking up to and my schedule has never been as busy!

> "STUDY THE SYSTEMS TO EVOLVE. THE BETTER YOU UNDERSTAND THE SYSTEM, THE LESS YOU WILL HAVE TO WORK."
>
> Dr. BAK NGUYEN

From there, your next stage will be to leverage the systems. That's what I did. I mastered one system then, another one. I did so again and again. Today, I am building and my blocs are the systems that I mastered. This is my version of laziness. Today, this is how I overachieve being lazy, because I am building higher and higher using the same pieces (systems).

In short, don't buy a coffee, buy *comfort* and *empowerment*. Thinking won't produce any hormones, so no leveraging. Feeling will. Feel good first and leverage your body to skip procrastination! If lazy people still have to work, make sure that you can leverage that same work many, many times over. This is what I meant by studying the systems.

And one last piece of advice before closing this chapter. Be your own financial advisor. People often ask who to trust about your finance. Your first and only answer should always be yourself! You work hard for your money, make sure to take control so eventually, your money will be working hard so you won't have to!

So what about your house? Well, buy that coffee first and learn a system as you are enjoying that coffee. Then, *spoil* yourself some more with travel or whatever makes you happy. Leverage that happiness. And if you spent much time studying the right system, buying your first house might not be an expanse but your first inventory!

This is **TO OVERACHIEVE EVERYTHING BEING LAZY**, the second volume of the LAZY franchise. Welcome to the Alphas.

CHEAT YOUR WAY TO SUCCESS
Dr. BAK NGUYEN

CHAPTER 5
HOW TO CHALLENGE YOUR NEGATIVE THOUGHTS?

"""THINK IT IS GOOD, THINK IT IS BAD, EITHER WAY, YOU ARE RIGHT!"
BY DR. BAK NGUYEN

I will start to say that I have no secret recipe for negative thoughts. We live in a society in which, to grow, we must be open to share vibes and information. If we are sending our inputs in society and to other people, this goes both ways. So there is no way to stop the vibe from coming in, good and bad.

That said, most of our negative thoughts, surprisingly, are not originating from the outside. A quick google search looking for the source of negative thoughts on google will bring you to the conclusion that circumstances is most often the minor share of what influence our happiness (the opposite of negative thoughts.

Some will advance that circumstances contribute to about 10% of our happiness while our *state of mind* (if trained, called mindset) will contribute for 40% and genetic, 50%. We can argue on the importance of each field, but one fact remains dominant: our perception of reality is the major shareholder of your thoughts.

In other words, negative thoughts often emerge from inside. Even those from the outside don't shift as drastically our thoughts, unless, we are looking actively for such stimulus.

"THINK IT IS GOOD, THINK IT IS BAD, EITHER WAY, YOU ARE RIGHT!"

I wish I could sign that quote! But really, you are always right. Your truth and reality depend on how you perceive the world and all the opportunities and risks coming your way. Let use another word for these two, challenge.

> "IF AN OPPORTUNITY AND A RISK WERE BOTH DIFFERENT FACES OF THE SAME COIN, CHALLENGE IS THE COIN."
>
> Dr. BAK NGUYEN

So what happens as you face any challenge. You will internalize the change and evaluate what has changed and what will affect you. The first thing that most people will do is to try to ignore that change until it reaches a critical threshold. We call that the *buffer zone*.

Until that point, no action or decision has been made yet, just our internalize information processing has been involved. Then, as the stimulus keeps pushing and triggers the threshold's alarm, we will start reacting. And reacting, by definition, we are always late.

How do you feel when you are behind the events? How do you feel when you are late? How do you feel when you have to run just to catch up? The common answer will be: not really good!

So how can one influence the negative thoughts coming from exterior circumstances? By lowering his or her threshold and reacting faster to the stimulus. The faster the reaction, the least the catching up. Make no mistake, you will still be running, but now, you might have a chance to be ahead!

Does this mean that people who react to every little change are ahead? We often qualify these people as paranoid and overreacting, not overachieving. They annoy most of us and are always discarded... until they are proven right. Fortunately, most of the time, they will be proven wrong. So no, I am not telling you to overreact, that will bring in even more stress and negativity. I am telling you that to be lazy, be proactive!

Keep your calm, we are still just in the information analyzing process, not in decision making. Analyze the changes and differences. Do that before it has the chance to push you to your boundaries. While you are still in your buffer zone, you are safe and calm. In other words, you have access to all of your capability and logic. This is where you are at your best.

Analyze as soon as you can and then, decide to act or not. Just do not discard everything until you reached your boundaries.

> **"ONCE YOUR BUFFER ZONE BURST,
> YOU WILL BE RUNNING, JUST TO CATCH UP!"**
> Dr. BAK NGUYEN

Doing so, any change might be an opportunity for you to surf the trend to further your situation. Jumping headfirst into the wave of your choosing will be a challenge but not a *dare* nor an *"I have no choice"* decision. And this is the upside.

Of course, no one can analyze all of the changes surrounding him or her. But once one is surfing a trend, he or she generates a new vibe. And as that vibe is growing in speed and importance, it creates a new *buffer zone*, one that is much larger than the initial *buffer zone*, allowing even more time and resources to interpret and react to the outside stimuli.

You wanted to be lazy, study first to gain the upper hand. As you are in control, in action, not just reacting, everything else becomes easier, because of the growth of your *buffer zone*. I study first and react as soon as I understand because the alternative is much, much more work with little to no upside.

> "YOU WANTED TO BE LAZY AND TO OVERACHIEVE,
> BE THE FIRST TO REACT AND BEFORE HAVING
> NO MORE CHOICE, LEAD THE TREND!"
>
> Dr. BAK NGUYEN

Easier said than done, will you say. Well, look at the alternative and decide for yourself. At least now, you know. Like anything else, this is a mindset that, if well mastered, becomes a state of mind: a second nature.

That is my mindset. But even though, I still have to face negative thoughts daily. Why? Because they only count for 10% of the sources of negative thoughts, those related to exterior circumstances. What about the other 90%?

Well, 40% is usually attributed to our mindset. In other words, how are we perceiving the world and 50% is, sit down for this one, 50% is related to genetics. Let's cover the genetic portion, shall we?

Are negative thoughts related to our genetics? Well yes. Self-doubt and confidence greatly influence how we feel. Consequently, our body will free the related hormonal response. Just like anything else in nature, we will be reacting to that internal stimuli. Repetition of the same stimuli over and over again will set up *patterns*. And these *patterns* will dictate our **reactions by default** to everything else.

Some, from genetics, will have natural ease to produce more or less hormones. This factor will be of great importance in the beginning but eventually, the *patterns* set will be of a much greater influence over our behaviours.

So yes, genetics is part of the game but repetition is a much greater contributor. That covers the genetic contribution. Unfortunately, on genetic, we do not have much power over it. What we can influence is the repetition. And that brings us to the last segment of importance of happiness/negative thoughts: our state of mind.

I told you that your body is reacting to exterior stimuli. How we react depends on how we perceived that stimulus in the first place. All changes, no matter how big or how small, will affect us. The only thing we can do is our timing to react to it. And within the timing, a challenge will define itself as an opportunity or a risk.

> "THE LATER ONE FACES A CHALLENGE,
> THE GREAT IS THE RATIO RISK/OPPORTUNITY."
> Dr. BAK NGUYEN

In other words, the odds of winning decrease exponentially with the procrastination one will sit on. The longer the procrastination, the fewer opportunities one will have. Please do not confuse laziness with procrastination. If anything, those procrastinating will only have to work twice as hard (or worse) to simply catch up.

> "BECAUSE I AM LAZY, I DO NOT PROCRASTINATE."
> Dr. BAK NGUYEN

And of course, just like any of you, I was not born that wise. I had my fair share of regrets and mistakes, missing the boat more than once. Even if my **Confidence** protects me from self-doubt most of the time, it is not a *foolproof shield*. So what do I do when I doubt, when I miss out when I am left behind?

I try to canalize what I feel: frustration, even fear. Instead of trying my best to dilute such feelings, I empower them with all of my strength. I empower my frustrations and fears to push my body to explode in an avalanche of hormones. And I stand ready to surf that storm to catch up and, hopefully, to come out ahead.

This is a great *cheat* to use as you are left behind. But be warned, it comes at a great cost. Even if I successfully generate momentums and tornadoes from my frustrations, the fuel I am burning were my emotions, the great and beautiful emotions I have inside of my heart.

Having done that more than once, I will keep that as a last resort solution. Today, I try to cherish my joy, hope, and innocence. This is what is shiny in my heart. What is left, I do not want to throw in the fire of frustration just to keep moving.

Today, I am pushing down procrastination to the blink of inexistence. I do not take lightly anything or anyone. I do not panic either since my *buffer zone* grew exponentially. And to remind myself not to face the wall of *"I have no choice"* once more, I leverage my laziness to be **proactive**, not reactive.

Because I have the time to think and see, I do not panic. Because I do not panic, I have a chance to gather all of myself and external resources to surf the changes and the trends ahead. I might be behind the events but, as a leader, I am often ahead in comparison to *Society* and *Conformity*.

Until an extinction-level change, I am surfing ahead and will be telling the story.

"A FACT IS A FACT, NEGATIVE OR POSITIVE, IT IS UP TO YOU TO DECIDE."
Dr. BAK NGUYEN

And the beauty of the equation is that as you are surfing, even and negative challenge, coming up ahead will transform your experience into, maybe the greatest opportunity of your life. But for that, you must get your feet wet. For that, you must be willing to jump headfirst.

Those are not dares, not even ambitions. The way I see it is that we will have to jump sooner or later. The only difference is that, the more you wait, the fewer upsides you will have from your jump. It is still the same jump!

"BE LAZY ENOUGH TO THROW PROCRASTINATION AWAY."

Dr. BAK NGUYEN

Now that you know the rules of the game of life, these rules that you are reacting to, what will be your next move? That discussion you must have, you will have, looking in the mirror. But here is another *cheat* to ease your way. Start with feeling, not with thinking.

Procrastination is not a feeling, it is a habit in your head. Don't think and you won't trigger it. Then, as you surf your emotions and hormones, procrastination will be nowhere near to be found. That to me, is the lazy way, the easy way.

> **"LAZY AND EASY, I LOVE THOSE WORDS.
> WITH THE RIGHT MINDSET, THEY WILL COME WITH WINS TOO!"**
> Dr. BAK NGUYEN

What a bold statement! Well, try it and write back to me. As many great minds wrote in the past, our greatest enemy is ourselves. Well, I will dare to modify that *fatality*.

> **"OUR GREATEST ENEMY IS THE IGNORANCE OF HOW WE ARE BUILT!"**
> Dr. BAK NGUYEN

Know who you are and start experiencing what you can do, what you can be. Negative or positive, those are still your thoughts. You can discard them or empower them. I say to leverage them all!

The answer is not in your head. The answer is not even in your heart. The true answer is always found in your *guts*. Take the time to acknowledge those sensations and do not confuse them with feelings (which are from the heart). If your head might lie to you and your heart might confuse you, your guts will never betray you. They are you!

You wanted to be lazy? To avoid having to sort through the crap, forget thinking. You want to be lazy and to react faster and faster, skip your heart and listen to your guts, from the beginning. Then, as you understood the message, go back up to your heart to know how to react according to your desires and values.

As you are shifting from information processing to decision making and into action, only then, go to your head. With your first move dictated from your guts and heart, you are now in trouble. Trust your head to get you out of that *mess*! It is how you will grow.

Doing so, negative and positive thoughts will both serve you as they are both generating hormones. Put those hormones into good use and start surfing the opportunities!

This is **TO OVERACHIEVE EVERYTHING BEING LAZY**, the second volume of the LAZY franchise. Welcome to the Alphas.

CHEAT YOUR WAY TO SUCCESS
Dr. BAK NGUYEN

CHAPTER 6
WHAT ABOUT EGO? CAN YOU LEVERAGE THAT TOO?

"ARE YOU LEVERAGING YOUR FEAR OR DESIRES, IT IS FOR YOU TO CHOOSE."
BY DR. BAK NGUYEN

Wow, what a great question, a tricky one! What about Ego? The obvious answer would be to drop your **EGO** to move forward light and free. But you are looking to be lazy and you are now looking for a *cheat*. Congratulation, you are starting to shift your words and, consequently, your mindset!

I was born with a huge **EGO** myself. I was also very loved, so very young, I learnt to care, genuinely for others. Every time I was successful in something, I would come home and share it with my parents.

My parents are immigrants. They work by day and study by night to regain the social status, pride, and the wealth that 2 wars stole from them. They do not have any time to spare for recognition. No matter how great I was doing, the best I could get from them was, what's next?

When I rebelled and pushed myself to score things no one in the family did before, they told me to stop bragging! I was labeled at a very young age as an *arrogant* and a rebel. *Arrogant* because I knew more and do more and, eventually refuse to learn from lesser people. Rebel because what they were looking for, not just my parents but my teachers and the whole education system, was for me to obey without questioning.

All of that strengthened my **EGO** but instead of fighting a never-ending fight, I gave up on them, them all. On the surface, I did what they wanted of me. I did not enjoy any minute of it but I delivered what was asked of me as fast and as soon as possible.

Of course, I wasn't good at it, but very quickly, I realized that the better I get at the task, the less of my time I needed to spend doing something I despise.

So I started listening in class, really listening. What else could I do, I was stuck there anyway! I was listening with the intention to get rid of the homework and exam coming. I knew that I won't have any recognition for from my parents but that stopped bothering me. I scored higher and higher because it was my easiest way out!

They thought that they have broken me, that I was conforming. They all did, my parents, my family, my teachers, my private school, the priests, and all of **Conformity**. Oh, I forgot to mention that I was raised in a very strict Catholic household. By 10, I knew much of the Bible inside and out! That did not help my case but not at all!

What I craved in recognition at home, I got from my fellow students. Because I was motivated to score, I was ahead within a very competitive scholar environment. I was not the brightest but my *ratio performance/time spent* was unbeatable! I was always the one who study the least and with higher than average results.

Most of my fellow students were aiming to score as high as possible, not me. I was looking for efficiency, to get rid of the task and to stay above the reproach, because if I did not have recognition, the blame and the guilt were very quick to fall as I came home with anything *sinking into the average…*

I love my parent dearly. They had to face a much harder life than I did. On that, I agree with my dad: I am building, standing from his shoulders. Succeeding at school on my own terms, built me up from the inside. I grew more and more *Confident*.

Not caring for the opinions of the other (I gave up on them, remember?) made me into a very independent thinker. I have my questions but I do not ask them in class. I look for their answers in the books and novels I found refuge in. Yes, those were my ways to escape my time in prison at school.

At home, when I got my first computer, I found a ground to simulate what I learnt from my books and questions. I learnt to strategize, to create and to adapt from video games.

To my teachers, I was an okay student, one performing but not too interested to push the boundaries. To most of them, I reached my place as a higher than average student, one with a flame in his eyes that did not cause too many troubles.

To my parents, I was not a problem anymore. They gave me all that they could and I was caring the *torch of hope* forward for a better future. Actually, I had on my shoulder the burden to prove them right, they bet everything on their children and I was the eldest!

And **EGO** in all of this? Well, because I was made stronger and stronger, I can hear but I won't obey. I delivered, not because I cared but because I wanted out. Things were harmonious for as long as we were not talking of anything that really matters.

I can stay silent but when they asked my opinion, I did not lying. That's how I was tattooed as arrogant on my forehead, from everyone, parents, family, fellow students, and teachers. I accepted that and I moved on.

Because I did not care, I was not hurt either. And then, I reached university and the graduation test of pride and immigration of my parents. As the eldest child in an immigrant family, the only way for me to regain the family honour was to have the letters D and R in front of my name.

I already told you, I love my parents with all of my heart, even if we do not get along. I will do anything for them. Well, I had to put my money where my mouth was. I became a D and R. But that in itself was not easy.

Back in college (CEGEP), I knew that only the first 3 sessions mattered to the selection process to recruit the next generations of future doctors, which is the top on the list of the desirable programs. It was like the chance to change social status in a lottery that you control the odds. Work hard, be better than the best and you might have a chance.

Well, my relative ease of studying got me to become overconfident. I did my usual, studying with a great *ratio effort/result* and got prepared for the admission of both medical and dental schools. For my parents, they did not care much, for as long as the letters were D and R.

Dental school was 4 years back then. Medical school was at least 7. What do you think that I went for? But not to hear more on the matter, I applied to both. Back then, the selection process was based on the Z curve. I verified and I was ahead and safe, compared to the 2 last years' statistics.

The selection process also required interviews in some universities. Usually, this is where the best students fail, lacking confidence and social skills. Well, those, I had more than required, my only concern was to get to the interview and to be myself there.

I worked hard all of my life to that point to please my parents and *Conformity*, I wanted to give into my **EGO** for once. I knew that I was ok for the selection process. All of my life, I was aiming at the best score possible with least time spent. What about aiming for the minimum with the least time spent?

At my 4 sessions in college, I showed up in class and kept my usual performance for about half of the semester. As I was sure that I was passing that course, I stopped showing up and went out to have fun. It was a great time in my life, flirting and enjoying my freedom (my parents were sure that I was studying at school)!

My average dropped about 20% by the last semester and I did not care at all! I got to my interview in dental school and score one of the best scores a student ever had in one of them! And then, I received a letter from the admission committee saying that I was on the waiting list. Was that an error?

I called the admission bureau and they informed me that the selection process changed from the Z curve to a new norm call R. The math was much, much different. That was the first time they applied it and anyone can feel their insecurity.

Long story short, I waited the whole summer, 14th in rank, waiting to receive my letter of admission. They stopped at 12! Most of my fellow students and friends went through the same deception but as they were aiming for medical school (which is much more demanding), as they failed, they got accepted into dental school or pharmacy school. I was aiming for dental school without any else to fall too!

I started University in biology, a redemption program to try readmission the following year. It was not only hard on me because I failed where most of my fellow students got saved with their backup. Sure, the morale was at its lowest but now, my 4th semester with that mediocre 20% down in average that I had to carry around! I screwed myself! Now, it was my **EGO** that pushed to keep going.

On top of that, DR programs are very specific, they have quotas for students fresh from college or with a bachelor's degree. For those in between, there isn't much chance. How could I come out ahead with the new R system and a drop of 20% in my average?

I studied the system and the selection process once more, hoping that this time, they will not change it anymore. I learnt that the ponderation of my time in University will be taken into account as such: 2% times the number of credits done.

Most of the students will have a session of 10 to 12 credits, this is what is considered a normal schedule. I push to have 16 credits. That time 2% will at least give me a chance to balance my mediocre fall of 20%.

I have to tell you that I have never worked as hard in my entire life. The Hell with the ratio of productivity, I was studying day and night, going only to the gym to train to release the frustration and to stay sane. I was miserable.

Once again, I knew that only my first semester will be taken into account. With all of my will and vital strength, I scored a 3.9 GPA. That got me again into the interview process. I was broken, if that one failed, I could not survive 2 more years of that…

I received my letter from the admission bureau. One year later after the first letter putting me in 14th position, this year, I was 5th in line, waiting for my admission to dental school.

The admission bureau gives you a telephone number to call to verify where they are at in the admission process. By June, they were at the 4th already. Usually, that would mean that I was sure to get in but last year taught me a very important lesson, nothing was ever sure.

I waited the whole summer. Maybe it was not meant to be. I was packing up my hope, pain, and deception and was ready to confront my parents. I was not cut for it. Then, the admission bureau sent a letter. I was admitted in pharmacy school!

Pharmacy, drugs, and chemistry, I hated those! Without saying much, I declined the offer. It was the only little victory I had for the last 12 months, to refuse instead of being refused. I was about to mail that letter to the admission bureau when my parents stumbled on the letter and my refusal… I was in, not for a long night but a week in hell.

I love my parents dearly but a year studying something meaningless to me showed me that I wasn't cut for this. I will shoot myself before graduation.

As we were arguing and that even my grandparents were now part of the discussion, the admission bureau sent another letter. I was accepted into dental school, finally! Needless to say what kind of celebrations followed. For once, my family and I, we were all agreeing on something!

Looking back at this episode of my life, 25 years later, I can still feel the pain and the doubt. But that year in exodus cut the fat of **EGO** from my personality. I kept my discipline for the first 2 months in dental school and quickly resumed my productivity ratio. Very soon, boredom will kick in.

Very briefly, in response to that boredom, I started an independent movie project and got myself into even more trouble. To graduate from dental school is hard enough, to do that and to do the impossible producing and directing an independent movie on top was *suicidal*.

This is a story for another book but in short, I got myself into much more trouble than I bargained for. It was my **EGO** that kept my head above the water. I refused to let all of my team and the people who believed in me, down.

Was that **EGO**? Of course, it was. I felt once, the look of the other looking down on me as I failed my admission the first time. Image the condescension with me failing either dental school or my side film project?

EGO alone did not save me. My love for others did. I successfully complete my dental program as I entered the clinical part and had patients to care for. With them, this was not about trying the best ratio but about getting them to the finish line as soon as possible and with as most ease as possible. They did not like to be there, me neither, on that we connected.

To help them, I needed to improve my skills and whatever I missed in class, I went to learn and mastered after hours. I was there for my patients. This is 25 years after the facts, trust me, it is not about looking good. That genuine connection with people kept me going and saved me from drowning from my dental journey.

On the other hand, so many people believed in me as I was launching the idea to make a film. I even received money from the Federation of Students to do so. This was not about me anymore but about keeping the promise made. I was heavily challenged, lost my film director halfway through the process. I was producing, never was it intended for me to direct, even less to edit. But this was not about technicality, it was about keeping my words with those who believed and invested in me.

My **EGO** kept me going and that dedication to keep going no matter what, inspired more and more people to join in and help. I finished that independent film as a first in the history of the University of Montreal, not just from the dental department but as a first across all departments. And, by the way, the University of Montreal has a movie-making department. That was in 2001, before the smartphones and the digital age.

Despite that my **EGO** saved me from drowning more than once, it was also responsible for most of my mistakes and challenges. Looking back, most of the difficulties that I met going forward, I put them, myself, on my head, some times from **EGO**, some times from ambitions.

I understood the concept of **EGO** only much, much later as 3 of my mentors told me how humble I was. Humble? Me? All of my life, I was *tattooed* as arrogant. Something that you have to know about my mentors, they can be kind but they are also very direct and will not spare my feelings with kind words.

Looking in their eyes, in all 3, I saw how they saw the humility in me. To them, being humble has nothing to do with my achievements, my ambitions, or how I communicate them. I was humbled because I was always open to listen and to learn.

Those who labeled me as *Arrogant*, they did so because they failed to get me to listen. Looking back, they too refuse to listen to anyone else but to those sharing their opinions and perspective. What they labelled me with was in fact meant for them... somehow.

> "ARROGANCE IS NOT THE RECOGNITION OF WHO WE ARE BUT THE DENIAL OF WHAT WE ARE NOT."
> Dr. BAK NGUYEN

Arrogance and *humility* are faces of **EGO**, of how we perceive ourselves. Well, know who you are and be open to learn. Learning, you will be growing. You still have to choose what you are learning. And the answer that you seek, you will only find it being *Confident*, being comfortable with yourself and your true desires.

From a young age, I learnt to not care about others' opinions. I do not care for their opinions but I do care for them. The letters of nobility D and R, made sure that I never forget that.

> "YOU CALL ME DOCTOR TO REMIND ME TO ALWAYS PUT YOUR NEEDS BEFORE MINE."
> Dr. BAK NGUYEN

And that is how I became influential and even powerful. The more people I helped, the more my influence grew. *Recognition* followed pretty soon. And of course, with *recognition* also came *jealousy*.

There are 2 kinds of people that will give you *recognition*: those you help to ease their pain and those who have something to gain to empower you. And *jealousy*? Well, those are from your peers and equals, those standing in line with you and running a similar race.

Your *recognitions* reminded them of what they haven't succeeded yet or have failed. They do not hate you, what they hate is the reflection of them that they see in you. And looking at them, it is even easier to understand what is **EGO**.

I had my definition of **EGO**, what about them? Well, what is **EGO** but to wrap your flaws and vulnerabilities with all of yourself and to keep it close to your heart? Take the time to unwrap what you hold in your **EGO** and see clearly.

You don't have to do it in public, do it in your comfort zone, looking truly into your soul. Find that flaw and ask yourself if you now want to wrap it back in your heart? Whatever your decision, it is okay, because now you have erased *arrogance*, you now know.

And **EGO** is nothing more than the *box*, close to the heart, in which we deposit what we decide. For some it will be ambitions, for others, it will be their desires, of others, it will be pleasures. **EGO** is that safe place to come to, to feel better. But some, to feel better, decide to hide inside of **EGO** their flaws, thinking that no one will see them.

Well, here's a secret. The *box of* **EGO** will amplify everything that you put inside. Close to the heart and with the blood pumping in, **EGO** will grow and empower whatever you have put in it.

> "ARE YOU LEVERAGING YOUR FEAR OR DESIRES, IT IS FOR YOU TO CHOOSE."
> Dr. BAK NGUYEN

And that is my take on **EGO**. It is neither good nor bad. **EGO** can save you from drowning but in most situations, it also put you there in the first place. Know what is **EGO** and understand how it works. Then, be aware of what you enclose within your **EGO**.

And how about that *cheat*? Well, **EGO** is so close to the heart. It can also infect the head. But **EGO** has no power over your guts, your instincts. Well, listen to your instincts first, listen to your needs and your decisions will be *ego-free*.

> "GENERATE YOUR HORMONES FROM YOUR NEEDS AND DESIRES, NOT YOUR FEARS."
> Dr. BAK NGUYEN

This journey is all about laziness. Well, study the systems first and leverage them to save yourself much harder work with little to no upside down the road.

This is **TO OVERACHIEVE EVERYTHING BEING LAZY**, the second volume of the LAZY franchise. Welcome to the Alphas.

CHEAT YOUR WAY TO SUCCESS
Dr. BAK NGUYEN

CHAPTER 7
HOW TO LOVE AND GROW?

"IF YOU WERE LOOKING FOR LOVE WITH A CAPITAL L, WELL, ATTRACTION IS A FAR BETTER WAY (LAZINESS WISE) TO ACTIVE SEEKING!"

BY DR. BAK NGUYEN

What are success and wealth good for if we have no one to share them with? In the first volume of this journey, you asked how to seduce your *crush*. Now, as we are in a relationship, how about love? If seducing your partner was a self-esteem challenge, loving is a whole other story.

> ### "LOVING IS ABOUT GIVING AND GROWTH."
> Dr. BAK NGUYEN

Nothing new here. Loving is about giving. But did you know that growth happens on the giving end? Ever heard that when you love someone, you are becoming a better person? Some will change to please that person. That will work for a while until the hormones shift and a confrontation of values become inevitable.

> ### "WE EVOLVE, WE DO NOT CHANGE."
> Dr. BAK NGUYEN

Changing will mean to erase the past and to build from scratch. No one is really doing that for love. If there are, they are living a lie, both in their romance and in their personal journey. The values, we all carry them inside. When we love, we are simply deciding which values to prioritize more. **Repetition** and **Time** will be doing the rest.

The longer we are empowering a value, an emotion, the more we are exposed to its *benefits* and *consequences*. Dealing with those, we are adapting our behaviours to that value. And, of course, the more we keep triggering the same stimuli, the more we will grow under its influence until it becomes a big part of who we are.

So how to apply laziness to love? Most of us will spend a lifetime looking for the perfect person. Some will find that special person and some are still looking. Some never gave up, even after decades of searching.

Well, if you ask me, I will start with what is easier. I will learn to love myself first. Not in the way you just picture! What I meant is that to love someone, we must first be comfortable with ourselves. What was the problem of looking for the perfect partner? We have to look for that person and we are not sure if that is the right person or not! Those are huge risks!

Since growth happens at the giving end, can we leverage that to grow and to define ourselves? What a great idea! But wait, I just said that we have to grow first and then find love…

Well, loving you are exposing yourself to be hurt. That everyone knows. But some loves are easier and more natural than others. The easiest will be to look for love in **GRATITUDE**. Everyone will tell you that being grateful is nice and good. How about leveraging that?

Give back to the people who loved and supported you. Give, do not try to convince them and to convert them to your point of view, just love them. The usual problem we are facing when facing our family and those we love, is that it is about *sharing*, not *giving*.

Well, giving is a one-way street while sharing goes both ways. By giving, you have to understand what the other person desires and craves for and to provide that. This will force you into listening mode and to forget about your own quest of identity for a little while.

Then, as you understood what the other person desire, you still need to deliver, forcing you to grow out of your comfort zone to materialize that desire. Well, do it first and write back to me. What just happen? It was easier to grow since this time, you have no identity issue, no *but*, no *if*, no should. Just a clear way to execute!

Executing, you are already shifting hormones into a *proactive mode*, you are feeling better already! And then, what is coming next is even more powerful. As you are making the other person happy, maybe even proud, what are the feelings and hormones that you are bathing in? You feel on top of the world, without *but*, *if* or *should*!

You accomplished that *without much resistance* (since it was not about you) and you had to outgrow yourself to deliver. As a result, you felt great the whole time travelling that path. What do you think you will do? You will repeat the process and grow even bigger, faster!

The danger here was to not distinguish between *giving* and *sharing*. If you go in, looking to share, you will be repeating the same pattern that pushed you away from those you love the most.

Trust me on that, I've been there more than once. They do not have to understand you, that's alright. You, on the other hand, took the time to understand their desire, without the interference of your *doubts* and *beliefs*.

So even if you took in the information, it was to materialize their desires. Nowhere on this timeline, your identity will be tested or even under attack. Your identity will only benefit from your own actions and will to listen first and to provide. This is how you grew *without resistance*.

> "TO GROW WITHOUT RESISTANCE IS THE FASTEST WAY TO GROW, EVEN IF THE JOURNEY IS AN NEVER-ENDING ONE."
> Dr. BAK NGUYEN

If you want a clear example of this, look at any woman as she is giving birth and becoming a mother. Before the birth of the baby, she is changing physically but her mindset hasn't shifted yet. She is still who she always was.

Then, as the baby is born, the exhausted mother will be submerged with a flow of hormones empowering her body to feel and to protect that newborn. Overnight, she now has twice the energy has had before, even if she does not sleep much.

The baby is hungry, she will feed her baby. The baby is cold, she will hold and nurture. The baby is asleep, she is contemplating. She gave and gave and gave, and yet, she is ready to give even more! This is how she grew overnight!

She grew not from her mindset but from the construct of her body responding to the hormonal stimuli. Well, I cannot tell you that I have experienced such transformation since I am a male but what I can tell you is to leverage **GRATITUDE**, you are recreating these conditions… as close as possible.

And who should you be grateful to? Start with your parents! Even if we know that the flow in life is forward, giving back to those who raised us is a direct hit for growth and good feelings. Then, as you are now more familiar with the process, you can broaden your *scope of Gratitude*.

I wasn't born as wise, so that took me a while before understanding the key difference between **GIVING** and **SHARING**. As I told you, I love my parents dearly but until I understood the *power of Giving*, I was *sharing*. At every turn, it was a fight! A fight to know who is in control, a fight to know who is right. A fight to know which step to take next.

> "TO EVERY ATTEMPT OF GRATITUDE, MY LOVE WAS PUT TO THE TEST, UNTIL I STOPPED SHARING AND STARTED GIVING."
>
> Dr. BAK NGUYEN

To be fair, I had my D-R title to thank for that. When I am helping a patient, it is not about me, not about my identity. It is all about understanding the other person's needs and to seek for a solution. I did that with *empathy*, putting myself in their shoes each time. Then, it was a matter of skillset (which I expand throughout the years), and voilà! Mission accomplished!

As one person was leaving happy, a new one came into my dental chair. And I repeated the process, listening and seeking solutions. Each person will present a unique set of *desires/problems*. As I put myself into their shoes, I felt their pain and hope, so I executed with sensitivity and kindness. That brought me success and recognition.

I got along with most of my patients but still, not as much with my family. With family, everything was complicated but love, that we were sure was there. Only when I stopped *sharing* and started *giving*, leveraging Gratitude that I successfully set the **EGO** of everyone apart. We could finally enjoy love without clouds.

There is an art to giving. There is an art to receiving. There is also an art to demanding. Each one is a different skill set and mindset to understand and to master. But if you were looking for a cheat, **LOVE** is your key!

I know that this was not what you expected from a chapter on love. Actually, we covered that already! Do not confused attraction (physiologic sexual hormonal response) with **Love**.

That still leaves us with a philosophical question: what is love? I am sure that we might find as many answers as we have people. I will let you find and forge your own.

> "AS FOR ME, LOVE IS TO GIVE. TO HAVE PEOPLE TO GIVE TO IS THE MOST PRECIOUS OF GIFTS."
> Dr. BAK NGUYEN

Once more, study the systems first, that will save you much, much harder work down the road. You don't like to study?

Fine, wait for your first challenge and study that challenge. Whatever you did to resolve the issues, do it again, this time, before facing a new problem.

So if you don't know who to love, stop asking the question. Look back at those who love you. Loving them and giving to them will have you experience the magic of love and you will be growing without resistance. As you are feeling great, you will be repeating the same process again and again, growing stronger, wiser, and kinder.

Oh yes, giving, you are growing kinder, your heart expanded to now include those under your love and care. Well, guess what, you are not the same person anymore. Growing as such and as much, you are now attracting much more people and potential partners to you.

And this is how I love myself! I leverage **Gratitude** to grow my **Confidence** and grow with much less resistance. Then, as it was easier since I was bathing in the right hormones, I pushed for more and more. Today, I don't have to seek love, I attract **Love**!

> "IF YOU WERE LOOKING FOR LOVE WITH A CAPITAL L, WELL, ATTRACTION IS A FAR BETTER WAY (LAZINESS WISE) TO ACTIVE SEEKING!"
>
> Dr. BAK NGUYEN

This is **TO OVERACHIEVE EVERYTHING BEING LAZY**, the second volume of the LAZY franchise. Welcome to the Alphas.

CHEAT YOUR WAY TO SUCCESS
Dr. BAK NGUYEN

CHAPTER 8
HOW TO DEFEND YOURSELF FROM MANIPULATIVE PEOPLE?

"TO UNCOVER MANIPULATION, AMPLIFY. IN EVERY DAY'S TERMS, EMPOWER PEOPLE."
BY DR. BAK NGUYEN

How to defend yourself from manipulative people? I hate that question of yours, not once but twice. First of all, to defend implies a weakness. If you start with the need to defend yourself, you are already putting yourself in a weak position. So what? Well, remember how the hormones work?

If you are feeling weaker, you are feeling insecure and your hormones will reflect that state of mind. This isn't positive or negative thinking. What do you think happens as your body is producing those stress hormones allowing you to flee (primal reaction built in your DNA)? Well, you are painting a *bullseye* on your back! This is the last message you want to communicate!

Feeling inferior and under attack will not result with the same chemical reactions from your body and therefore, what you are feeling and your decision process will also be altered by your perception. Don't start by putting yourself in a position of weakness, it is always harder to come back from there. I am not talking about bragging or being overconfident, I am talking about the hormones your will be generating.

That was the first reason why I hated your question. The second is that you use the word *manipulate*. Once again, you are acting as a *victim* and you are closing yourself up. Let's make something clear, everybody has an agenda and every, just like you, they are working for their own interests. There is nothing wrong with that.

That said, how can you grow if you have a screen and a shield to sort out most people looking to connect with you, in other words, to sell you something. Since everyone is looking to sell you something, those who will pass your sorting system are just better hiding their intentions.

You are lying to yourself and will surround yourself with master manipulators and liars, thinking that you are safe. To me, this is surely not a smart nor lazy way to advance in your journey.

> "EACH AND EVERYONE HAS AN AGENDA. IT DOES NOT MEAN THAT WE CAN JOIN FORCES AND WORK TOGETHER."
>
> Dr. BAK NGUYEN

This is what saying **YES** to everything within 18 months taught me. I needed a way to reboot my sorting system and to let go of the hypocrisy, the jealousy, and the lies. That being said, I did not know where to start. The simplest solution was to get rid of the *gate*.

I met all kinds of people. Some ok, some good, some great, and some plain bad. Did I lose more time and energy than before (when I had my *gates of elitism* up)? Actually, I gain in speed and became much stronger opening up to everyone.

Yes, I got hurt, but not as bad as before, when people betrayed my trust. Yes, some tried to manipulate me, I held back and observed. Eventually, I saw enough and present them with a mirror of themselves. It did not take long for them to disappear.

Opening up also brought to me the opportunity to meet with great people I would not have met under different circumstances. 2 of my good friends and mentors today are amongst the most respected and influential people in their field at a national level.

Well, I wanted to change my life, so I need to welcome change, starting with the people I was talking with. Later on, that same openness got me to meet with a great American inventor who created MLS (multi-listing system) the backbone of today's real estate market. The same man also digitalized Wall Street's bond market. If I was not open, I would only be reading about these people from books and magazines!

And what about their agenda? I told you before, everyone has an agenda. Even people looking to help you are looking for an angle for them to win. That is ok. You have to make your peace with that. Those hypocrites are those saying that they do not want anything in return and will be stealing behind your back.

So if you want a *cheat* here, look for what the other person has to gain. *"Follow the money!"* to borrow from common wisdom. The more straightforward people are with you, the more you can trust them. Once that is established, you can develop a trust relationship and friendship that might be mutually beneficial.

> "KEEP IN MINE THAT RELATIONSHIPS ARE A TWO-WAY STREETS. WHATEVER IS ONE-WAY, IS EITHER SHORT TERMS OR A LIE."
> Dr. BAK NGUYEN

I accepted a long time ago that everyone has their agenda. If I can, I will even help them to reach their goals. I am also very transparent about mine too. Being lazy, what I appreciate is honesty. Without honesty, there can be no trust. And to me, no trust means no go, even if they are promising the moon. I am open, not dumb.

I keep my friends happy and for the long term as we are straight with one another and are looking for ways to *pull our cards* together to win big. This is what I called synergy. And I can confirm to you that most of the time, a problem can seem complicated but once broken down into smaller pieces, we now have a plan of action.

From that plan of action, I may have a few pieces of the puzzle. My friends may have a few more. This is when we are *pulling our cards* together. And whatever missing, well, that may be half of the *puzzle* but look at the bright side, we already solve half of the problem already.

So am I happy to understand my partners' motivations? Absolutely, that helps me to address only the right people, not trying to convince them or to sell them anything, just looking to connect the dots.

For those looking to *B-S* me to manipulate me, well, as comes the time to put our cards on the table, you are calling these *bluffs*. Then, have enough courage to see the truth and to react to it, even if you call them friends and believed in their promises!

When this happens, and it will, it will hurt, really bad. Well, my *cheat* is to push for the moment to show all hands as soon as possible. This is the best way to limit your exposure and pain.

"TO UNCOVER MANIPULATION, AMPLIFY. IN EVERYDAY'S TERMS, EMPOWER PEOPLE."

Dr. BAK NGUYEN

If you were looking for a clear answer to face manipulative people, empower them. **To empower is to amplify**. And once you are amplifying, there is nowhere to hide, the card will fold quickly and the *real faces* will show. Now, before doing so, know that we each have our own agenda. That does not make all of us into manipulative people.

I am sure that to define manipulation, we might have, once again, as many definitions as we have people. Let's stick with what I know. Some of full of shit. Those are the ones manipulating people, selling you back your own resources. Spot them as soon as possible and deal with them accordingly.

About the others, it is a matter of trade. Some will trade their time, some, their assets, some their skills, some knowledge and information. For as long as you understand what you are buying and from *whom* (this is as important as what you are buying), you are doing good.

And why is by *whom* so important? Well, trade is base on trust and fairness. How can you trust if you do not know who is selling to you? And here comes the *key to this cheat*: you must know the other players on the table. Look for what triggers them and you might have a way to trade with them.

You too, have your agenda. This is the first time that every coach will tell you to sort out: what is your goal? I don't know about you but as a lazy guy, studying the systems, studying the people, that sounds like much, much work. But it is still much better than the alternative which will be to make mistakes and to run to fix them.

If you want a *cheat*, I look at **people** and **society** as a *poker game*. I have my cards, I know the rules, now it is about reading the other players. Well, guess what? Everyone is looking to win! That was easy. Knowing that, you can start studying **how** and **what** they are doing to win. You just learn to read that person.

Then, comes another person, and another. You will have to read each of them. Learning to read people in a poker game is not as hard as you might think. Especially since it is a game, you might enjoy your simulation and exercises.

Here's your *cheat*: in real life, most people are really bad *poker players* and their *poker faces* can be spotted miles around, if you knew what to look for. And reading people, you are not manipulative, you just know who are!

This is what I am doing on the ground, reading people with *poker skills*. Now, as a leader, my everyday job is to lead people and manage to coordinate all the efforts to achieve common goals.

To do that, I have to understand the other parties, to understand their agendas and what they are looking for. Then, my next question is to know how I can empower them to reach their goal.

Usually, by helping them to reach their goal, they will help me to reach mine. Am I a manipulative person? Not at all. People, from CEOs to students, are lining up for my help.

The next phase of the game, now that I have assembled and motivated my team, it is now about how to move forward. This won't be a poker game anymore but a *poker game combined with a chess game*. And this would be the subject of a whole other book.

This is **TO OVERACHIEVE EVERYTHING BEING LAZY**, the second volume of the LAZY franchise. Welcome to the Alphas.

CONCLUSION
BY DR. BAK NGUYEN

This is yet, another journey ending. This one was great, one started 14 chapters ago in volume one. I must say that I did not expect to have that much to say as I put myself in your shoes, in the shoes of millennials

Just like everyone else, you have the right to make your own mistake and to grow from them. That I know too much to tell you otherwise. That being said, I still believe that it does not have to be hard. I am a believer of short, sweet, and easy.

Looking back at my own journey, I had a lot of fun, made so many mistakes and I grew surviving each of them. Today, the scars on my back all tell a unique story. Would I love to cheat my way out of these? Absolutely! This is why I wrote these 2 books: **LAZY** volume 1 and 2.

This is mainly all I would have loved to know walking in your shoes. It will not save you from making your own mistakes but I am sure, it will help you to map the journey ahead. If I was in your shoes, I will be making my own choices and mistakes too but having read what will be coming, it will help me to fall back on my feet much faster.

To tell you the truth, I think that I would have made different mistakes, saving myself from the more basic ones. I am saying that because today, I am still making new mistakes. At each new mistake, there is a new lesson. That's how we all grow.

The sad thing is that we have been conditioned to think that mistakes are bad and that we have to avoid them at all cost. This is setting all of us back, by much, very much. How? Do you remember how our body is reacting as we feel insecure, in danger, or inferior? We are producing hormones accordingly, so we feel physically insecure, in danger, and inferior!

Well, to be fearful is one of the strongest triggers our body reacts to. There are enough challenges to terrify us out there, we do not need any new ones. So we are afraid of trying. To be afraid of making our mistakes also means to be afraid of learning and of change. In other words, it means to be **afraid of evolving**.

This is how **Conformity** screwed all of us, having us believe that mistakes are bad. A mistake is an experience. A mistake is to live. And from mistakes, we grow. So even if my intention was to save you from making your own mistakes, it would not be fair to expect that from you.

I am not saying that you will be running to your mistakes, I am saying that you have the right to live them and to earn them. This is how you experience life. That said, I like to think that I have eased your journey, telling you that you are not alone and that knowing that it was perfectly normal to learn from that mistake.

My intentions were not to save you from these mistakes or to strip you of your free choices. My intention was to help set your hormones right, so they served you. To have the right triggers, to generate the right hormones, and to leverage them to do whatever desires you have, those were my intentions.

I just showed you much power, even superpower if you put the knowledge in this book to good use. Please enjoy your newly found powers with **kindness** and the **respect** of others in mind. If you think that you just gain super strengths and that you can now step on people, you just miss out on even more power.

I told you that after leveraging my hormones to empower my desires, I started empowering the desires and needs of others. Well, I became much, much more influential since. *Less resistance and more influence,* that's my lazy formula.

"NOWADAYS, INFLUENCE IS POWER WITHOUT LIABILITY."

Dr. BAK NGUYEN

To evolve without *resistance* is the fastest way to evolve. It is the laziest way to evolve. To have power without liability is the most powerful of power since you keep your freedom.

> "I TOLD YOU THAT EVERYTHING IN LIFE IS A TRADE.
> BE CAREFUL OF WHAT YOU ARE TRADING."
> Dr. BAK NGUYEN

You have no idea how much I envy you. Your stories, your adventure, your growth. This is your life, enjoy every minute of it. And as you are ready to speed up, to do a little more, to be a little more, a little better, you now have all your body and hormones to leverage, being lazy!

From the bottom of my heart, I wish you nothing but the best life has to offer. Enjoy every minute of your journey! It is not over until it is over!

This is **TO OVERACHIEVE EVERYTHING BEING LAZY**, the second volume of the LAZY franchise. Welcome to the Alphas.

ABOUT THE AUTHORS

From Canada, **Dr BAK NGUYEN**, Nominee Ernst and Young Entrepreneur of the year, Grand Homage Lys DIVERSITY, and LinkedIn & TownHall Achiever of the year. Dr Bak is a cosmetic dentist, CEO and founder of Mdex & Co. His company is revolutionizing the dental field. Speaker and motivator, he wrote 72 books over 36 months accumulating many world records (to be officialized).

- **ENTREPRENEURSHIP**
- **LEADERSHIP**
- **QUEST OF IDENTITY**
- **DENTISTRY AND MEDICINE**
- **PARENTING**
- **CHILDREN BOOKS**
- **PHILOSOPHY**

In 2003, he founded Mdex, a dental company upon which in 2018, he launched the most ambitious private endeavour to reform the dental industry, Canada wide. Philosopher, he has close to his heart the quest of happiness of the people surrounding him, patients and colleagues alike. In 2020, he launched an International collaborative initiative named **THE ALPHAS** to share knowledge and for Entrepreneurs and Doctors to thrive through the Greatest Pandemic and Economic depression of our time.

In 2016, he co-found with Tranie Vo, Emotive World Incorporated, a tech research company to use technology to empower happiness and sharing. U.A.X. the ultimate audio experience is the landmark project on which the team is advancing, utilizing the technics of the movie industry and the advancement in ARTIFICIAL INTELLIGENCE to save the book industry and to upgrade the continuing education space.

These projects have allowed Dr Nguyen to attract interests from the international and diplomatic community and he is now the center of a global discussion in the wellbeing and the future of the health profession. It is in that matter that he shares his thoughts and encourages the health community to share their own stories.

"It's not worth it go through it alone! Together, we stand, alone, we fall."

Motivational speaker and serial entrepreneur, philosopher and author, from his own words, Dr Nguyen describes himself as a dentist by circumstances, an entrepreneur by nature and a communicator by passion.

He also holds recognitions from the Canadian Parliament and the Canadian Senate.

www.DrBakNguyen.com

AMAZON - BARNES & NOBLE - APPLE BOOKS - KINDLE
SPOTIFY - APPLE MUSIC

ULTIMATE AUDIO EXPERIENCE

A new way to learn and enjoy Audiobooks. Made to be entertaining while keeping the self-educational value of a book, UAX will appeal to both auditive and visual people. UAX is the blockbuster of the Audiobooks.

UAX will cover most of Dr Bak's books, and is now negotiating to bring more authors and more titles to the UAX concept. Now streaming on Spotify, Apple Music and available for download on all major music platforms. Give it a try today!

AMAZON - BARNES & NOBLE - APPLE BOOKS - KINDLE
SPOTIFY - APPLE MUSIC

COMBO
PAPERBACK/AUDIOBOOK
ACTIVATION

Please register your book to receive the link to your audiobook version. Register at: https://baknguyen.com/to-overachieve-everything-being-lazy-registry

Your license of the audiobook allows you to share with up to 3 peoples the audiobook contained at this link. Book published by Dr. Bak publishing company. Audiobook produced by Emotive World Inc. Copyright 2020, All right reserved.

FROM THE SAME AUTHOR
Dr Bak Nguyen

www.DrBakNguyen.com

MAJOR LEAGUES' ACCESS

FACTEUR HUMAIN -035
LE LEADERSHIP DU SUCCÈS
par Dr. BAK NGUYEN & CHRISTIAN TRUDEAU

ehappyPedia -038
THE RISE OF THE UNICORN
BY Dr. BAK NGUYEN & Dr. JEAN DE SERRES

CHAMPION MINDSET -039
LEARNING TO WIN
BY Dr. BAK NGUYEN & CHRISTOPHE MULUMBA

THE RISE OF THE UNICORN 2 -076
eHappyPedia
BY Dr BAK NGUYEN & Dr JEAN DE SERRES

BRANDING DrBAK -044
BALANCING STRATEGY AND EMOTIONS
BY Dr. BAK NGUYEN

002 - **La Symphonie des Sens**
ENTREPREUNARIAT
par Dr. BAK NGUYEN

006 - **Industries Disruptors**
BY Dr .BAK NGUYEN

007 - **Changing the World from a dental chair**
BY Dr. BAK NGUYEN

008 - **The Power Behind the Alpha**
BY TRANIE VO & Dr. BAK NGUYEN

036 - **SELFMADE**
GRATITUDE AND HUMILITY
BY Dr. BAK NGUYEN

072 - **THE U.A.X. STORY**
THE ULTIMATE AUDIO EXPERIENCE
BY Dr. BAK NGUYEN

088 - **CRYPTOCONOMICS 101**
MY PERSONAL JOURNEY
FROM 50K TO 1 MILLION
BY Dr BAK NGUYEN

BUSINESS

SYMPHONY OF SKILLS -001
BY Dr. BAK NGUYEN

CHILDREN'S BOOK
with William Bak

The Trilogy of Legends

THE LEGEND OF THE CHICKEN HEART -016
LA LÉGENDE DU COEUR DE POULET -017
BY Dr. BAK NGUYEN & WILLIAM BAK

THE LEGEND OF THE LION HEART -018
LA LÉGENDE DU COEUR DE LION -019
BY Dr. BAK NGUYEN & WILLIAM BAK

THE LEGEND OF THE DRAGON HEART -020
LA LÉGENDE DU COEUR DE DRAGON -021
BY Dr. BAK NGUYEN & WILLIAM BAK

WE ARE ALL DRAGONS -022
NOUS TOUS, DRAGONS -023
BY Dr. BAK NGUYEN & WILLIAM BAK

THE 9 SECRETS OF THE SMART CHICKEN -025
LES 9 SECRETS DU POULET INTELLIGENT -026
BY Dr. BAK NGUYEN & WILLIAM BAK

THE SECRET OF THE FAST CHICKEN -027
LE SECRETS DU POULET RAPIDE -028
BY Dr. BAK NGUYEN & WILLIAM BAK

THE LEGEND OF THE SUPER CHICKEN -029
LA LÉGENDE DU SUPER POULET -030
BY Dr. BAK NGUYEN & WILLIAM BAK

031- **THE STORY OF THE CHICKEN SHIT**
032- **L'HISTOIRE DU CACA DE POULET**
BY Dr. BAK NGUYEN & WILLIAM BAK

033- **WHY CHICKEN CAN'T DREAM?**
034- **POURQUOI LES POULETS NE RÊVENT PAS?**
BY Dr. BAK NGUYEN & WILLIAM BAK

057- **THE STORY OF THE CHICKEN NUGGET**
083- **HISTOIRE DE POULET: LA PÉPITE**
BY Dr. BAK NGUYEN & WILLIAM BAK

082- **CHICKEN FOREVER**
084- **POULET POUR TOUJOURS**
BY Dr BAK NGUYEN & WILLIAM BAK

THE SPIES AND ALIENS COLLECTION

077- **THE VACCINE**
079- **LE VACCIN**
077B- **LA VACUNA**
BY Dr BAK NGUYEN & WILLIAM BAK
TRANSLATION BY BRENDA GARCIA

DENTISTRY

PROFESSION HEALTH - TOME ONE -005
THE UNCONVENTIONAL
QUEST OF HAPPINESS
BY Dr. BAK NGUYEN, Dr. MIRJANA SINDOLIC,
Dr. ROBERT DURAND AND COLLABORATORS

HOW TO NOT FAIL AS A DENTIST -047
BY Dr. BAK NGUYEN

SUCCESS IS A CHOICE -060
BLUEPRINTS FOR HEALTH
PROFESSIONALS
BY Dr. BAK NGUYEN

RELEVANCY - TOME TWO -064
REINVENTING OURSELVES TO SURVIVE
BY Dr. BAK NGUYEN & Dr. PAUL OUELLETTE AND
COLLABORATORS

MIDAS TOUCH -065
POST-COVID DENTISTRY
BY Dr. BAK NGUYEN, Dr. JULIO REYNAFARJE AND
Dr. PAUL OUELLETTE

THE POWER OF DR -066
THE MODERN TITLE OF NOBILITY
BY Dr. BAK NGUYEN, Dr. PAVEL KRASTEV AND
COLLABORATORS

QUEST OF IDENTITY

004- **IDENTITY**
THE ANTHOLOGY OF QUESTS
BY Dr. BAK NGUYEN

011- **HYBRID**
THE MODERN QUEST OF IDENTITY
BY Dr. BAK NGUYEN

LIFESTYLE

045- **HORIZON, BUILDING UP THE VISION**
VOLUME ONE
BY Dr. BAK NGUYEN

048- **HORIZON, ON THE FOOTSTEPS OF TITANS**
VOLUME TWO
BY Dr. BAK NGUYEN

068- **HORIZON, DREAMING OF TRAVELING**
VOLUME THREE
BY Dr. BAK NGUYEN

MILLION DOLLAR MINDSET

MOMENTUM TRANSFER -009
BY Dr. BAK NGUYEN & Coach DINO MASSON

LEVERAGE -014
COMMUNICATION INTO SUCCESS
BY Dr. BAK NGUYEN AND COLLABORATORS

HOW TO WRITE A BOOK IN 30 DAYS -042
BY Dr. BAK NGUYEN

POWER -043
EMOTIONAL INTELLIGENCE
BY Dr. BAK NGUYEN

HOW TO WRITE A SUCCESSFUL BUSINESS PLAN -049
BY Dr BAK NGUYEN & ROUBA SAKR

MINDSET ARMORY -050
BY Dr. BAK NGUYEN

MASTERMIND, 7 WAYS INTO THE BIG LEAGUE -052
BY Dr. BAK NGUYEN & JONAS DIOP

PLAYBOOK INTRODUCTION -055
BY Dr. BAK NGUYEN

PLAYBOOK INTRODUCTION 2 -056
BY Dr. BAK NGUYEN

062- **RISING**
TO WIN MORE THAN YOU ARE AFRAID TO LOSE
BY Dr. BAK NGUYEN

067- **TORNADO**
FORCE OF CHANGE
BY Dr. BAK NGUYEN

071- **BOOTCAMP**
BOOKS TO REWRITE MINDSETS INTO WINNING STATES OF MIND
BY Dr. BAK NGUYEN

078- **POWERPLAY**
HOW TO BUILD THE PERFECT TEAM
BY Dr. BAK NGUYEN

PARENTING

024- **THE BOOK OF LEGENDS**
BY Dr. BAK NGUYEN & WILLIAM BAK

041- **THE BOOK OF LEGENDS 2**
BY Dr. BAK NGUYEN & WILLIAM BAK

086- **THE BOOK OF LEGENDS 3**
THE END OF THE INNOCENCE AGE
BY Dr. BAK NGUYEN & WILLIAM BAK

PERSONAL GROWTH

REBOOT -012
MIDLIFE CRISIS
BY Dr. BAK NGUYEN

HUMILITY FOR SUCCESS -051
BALANCING STRATEGY AND EMOTIONS
BY Dr. BAK NGUYEN

THE ENERGY FORMULA -053
BY Dr. BAK NGUYEN

AMONGST THE ALPHA -058
BY Dr. BAK NGUYEN & COACH JONAS DIOP

AMONGST THE ALPHA vol.2 -059
ON THE OTHER SIDE
BY Dr. BAK NGUYEN & COACH JONAS DIOP

THE 90 DAYS CHALLENGE -061
BY Dr. BAK NGUYEN

EMPOWERMENT -069
BY Dr BAK NGUYEN

THE MODERN WOMAN -070
TO HAVE IT HAVE WITH NO SACRIFICE
BY Dr. BAK NGUYEN & Dr. EMILY LETRAN

ALPHA LADDERS -075
CAPTAIN OF YOUR DESTINY
BY Dr BAK NGUYEN & JONAS DIOP

080- **1SELF**
REINVENT YOURSELF
FROM ANY CRISIS
BY Dr BAK NGUYEN

THE LAZY FRANCHISE

089- **THE CONFESSION OF
A LAZY OVERACHIEVER**
BY Dr BAK NGUYEN

090- **TO OVERACHIEVE
EVERYTHING BEING LAZY**
CHEAT YOUR WAY TO SUCCESS
BY Dr BAK NGUYEN

PHILOSOPHY

003- **LEADERSHIP** -003
PANDORA'S BOX
BY Dr. BAK NGUYEN

015- **FORCES OF NATURE**
FORGING THE CHARACTER
OF WINNERS
BY Dr BAK NGUYEN

040- **KRYPTO**
TO SAVE THE WORLD
BY Dr. BAK NGUYEN & ILYAS BAKOUCH

ALPHA LADDERS 2 -081
SHAPING LEADERS AND ACHIEVERS
BY Dr BAK NGUYEN & BRENDA GARCIA

MIRROR -085
BY Dr BAK NGUYEN

SOCIETY

LE RÊVE CANADIEN -013
D'IMMIGRANT À MILLIONNAIRE
par DR BAK NGUYEN

CHOC -054
LE JARDIN D'EDITH
par DR BAK NGUYEN

AFTERMATH -063
BUSINESS AFTER THE GREAT PAUSE
BY Dr BAK NGUYEN & Dr ERIC LACOSTE

TOUCHSTONE -073
LEVERAGING TODAY'S
PSYCHOLOGICAL SMOG
BY Dr BAK NGUYEN & Dr KEN SEROTA

COVIDCONOMICS -074
THE GENERATION AHEAD
BY Dr BAK NGUYEN

THE POWER OF YES

010 - **THE POWER OF YES**
VOLUME ONE: IMPACT
BY Dr BAK NGUYEN

037 - **THE POWER OF YES 2**
VOLUME TWO: SHAPELESS
BY Dr BAK NGUYEN

046 - **THE POWER OF YES 3**
VOLUME THREE: LIMITLESS
BY Dr BAK NGUYEN

087 - **THE POWER OF YES 4**
VOLUME FOUR: PURPOSE
BY Dr BAK NGUYEN

091 - **THE POWER OF YES 5**
VOLUME FIVE: ALPHA
BY Dr BAK NGUYEN

092 - **THE POWER OF YES 6**
VOLUME SIX: PERSPECTIVE
BY Dr BAK NGUYEN

TITLES AVAILABLE AT
www.DrBakNguyen.com

AMAZON - BARNES & NOBLE - APPLE BOOKS - KINDLE
SPOTIFY - APPLE MUSIC

www.ingramcontent.com/pod-product-compliance
Lightning Source LLC
Chambersburg PA
CBHW071511150426
43191CB00009B/1483